About Mary Kingston

Mary Kingston is a presenter with RTÉ's children's television and for the last five years she has been sharing her *Fantastic Far-Flung Facts for Fun* with us on Sunday's 'The Disney Club'.

Mary K grew up in Inchydoney, an island off the coast of West Cork. She lived in a house called 'Atlantic Haven' with her Mum, Dad, four sisters and three brothers, her dogs called Tiny and Scamper and Clarence the cat. Every day, when Mary K woke up, she saw the huge Atlantic Ocean from her bedroom. Every night, when Mary K went to sleep, she could hear the gentle waves crashing off the rocks at the edge of the huge Atlantic Ocean. While she slept, she dreamt that one day she would pack a small rucksack, a banana sandwich and put her camera around her neck to travel across every ocean to every continent to find out some *Fantastic Far-Flung Facts for Fun*. Mary K has travelled to every continent; on the way she has collected bizarre and brilliant facts about the animals of Africa, the myths and temples of Asia, and the deserts and reptiles of South America, and much, much more . . .

Mary K gets herself into all sorts of adventure on her travels. All travellers are advised to seek expert local help to stay safe.

BRIAN

This book is dedicated to Brian, the love of my life. Thank you for always reacting with such enthusiasm to every suggested destination and adventure.

A big
thank you

To all the people I met in all the fun, far-flung places, who shared their fantastic facts with me.
RTÉ: The Disney Club Team: John Keogh, Patricia Masterson, Nuala Malone, Marie Dorgan, Vicky Curtis, Hilary Jones, Niamh Guckian Ahern, Oliver Murphy, Finín O Ceallacháin and Oisín; Ray McCarthy 'cos 'You don't lick a book off the stones.'; The Galapagos Gang: Thank you for never, ever telling the dolphin/puke story; Marion Creely the producer, Stephen Spoor the underwater cameraman and Tom Curran the cameraman and Kevin Linehan for saying, 'The Galapagos? Off you go.' Birthe Tonseth, 'We'll always have Madagascar.' Greenland: The one and only Arctic Fox. Thanks Kathy Fox for the big trip and the little secret. CEL: Sinéad O'Connor and Claire O'Sullivan for their support. And thanks to all the gang in Young People's Programmes, RTÉ.

The publishers: Thanks to Michael O'Brien, Íde ní Laoghaire, Susan Houlden and Sinéad McKenna and all at The O'Brien Press for creating this fantastic book to give to my grandchildren – I love it.

A special mention to: Birdy Hickie, Teresa Smith, Michael Sheridan, Katie, Paul and Gabriel Weston, Aoileann Garavaglia, Pearse Lehane, Kevin O'Connell, Steve Curran, Geri Mae, Cormac Duffy, my godson Joseph Ryan, Sr Mary Killeen of Nairobi, Seán Farrell of Maynooth, David Moran, Kitty and Mike Waterer and escorted tours of Heathrow car parks, Séamas Hanrahan and Peter Moreton.

And finally thanks to: My Kingston family and all the long, long journeys and the sing-songs in the Blue Bus. A big thanks to Mum and Dad, Anne, Liam, Catherine, Denny, Johnny, Lou and Spud; to Lucky Dog in Inchydoney; Nelly Kingston for living faraway, all the better to visit you; Eric and Conor, but a special thanks to my Bangladeshi travelling companion, my goddaughter, Aisling Dineen aged two-and-a-half; for my nieces and nephews, Hannah Kingston, Ellen and Amy Beechinor, Aisling and Conor Dineen, Amy, Lauren, Scott, Jack and Robyn Graham; the Graham family for giving me a travelling companion, my Brian; Liz Scully and the first African adventure and the travel bug that has never been cured.

For all who put a rucksack on their backs and travel to meet people and visit places faraway with an open mind. And here's to everyone who reads this book for fun.

AISLING

Fantastic Far-Flung Facts for Fun

Mary Kingston

THE O'BRIEN PRESS
DUBLIN

RTÉ

First published 2004 by The O'Brien Press Ltd.,
20 Victoria Road,
Dublin 6,
Ireland.
Tel: +353 1 4923333; Fax: +353 1 4922777
E-mail: books@obrien.ie
Website: www.obrien.ie

ISBN: 0-86278-905-2

British Library Cataloguing-in-Publication Data
Kingston, Mary
Fantastic far-flung facts for fun
1.Curiosities and wonders - Juvenile literature
I.Title
032'.02

1 2 3 4 5 6
04 05 06 07 08

Photograph credits
Mary Kingston © all photographs except: p1, courtesy of Oliver Murphy and Victoria Curtis;
pp8-9 middle, © Dorling Kindersley; pp12-3 middle,
© National Geographic; pp14-5 middle, pp22-3 middle, p27 right
© Getty Images; pp28-9 middle, © Bruce Coleman Limited; p28 top and p31 bottom,
© ardea.com

Editing: The O'Brien Press Ltd
Design: Sinéad McKenna of Sin É Design
Illustrations of Mary K: David Moran
Cover photographs: Mary Kingston, except photograph of Mary Kingston on front cover,
courtesy of Oliver Murphy and Victoria Curtis
Printing: GraphyCEMS

Contents

Africa

Africa is the second largest continent in the world after Asia and is home to the fastest, tallest and largest land animals! The people are musical, colourful, fun and very laid back. One of their favourite sayings is 'hakuna matata', which means 'no worries'.

Madagascar

Mad about Madagascar

Madagascar is a unique and exotic island, which lies off the coast of East Africa. The first settlers were the Malay-Polynesians, who migrated from South-East Asia, bringing their food, music and traditions.

Noro, aged 6

The carnivorous pitcher plant – 'Look out, Mr Fly!'

Mary K Fun Facts

Madagascar, the fourth largest island in the world, is home to:

- 🐾 The world's population of lemurs.
- 🐾 50% of all the world's species of chameleon.
- 🐾 The carnivorous pitcher plant.
- 🐾 The giant jumping rat (gross!).

What's a reptile?

Reptiles have a bony skeleton and dry, scaly skin, which protects them from drying out and damage. They are cold-blooded creatures so they need the sun and warm surfaces to keep warm.

Turtles and tortoises

Turtles and tortoises are the world's oldest reptiles. Tortoises are reptiles with shells. Their shells protect them from their enemies and bad weather, but these shells also make them terribly slow. This land tortoise, the radiated tortoise of Madagascar, is endangered.

Do turtles have teeth?

Turtles do not have teeth but they have a strong beak for feeding on vegetation or coral. Like birds, turtles lay eggs; their eggs are leathery, elastic and soft.

The cutest lizard in Madagascar

Lizards are the largest and most widespread group of reptiles. They have slim bodies, large heads, four legs, a long tail and little beady bright eyes. Geckos are swift, agile lizards, which can camouflage among the trees of the rainforest.

How do geckos walk upside down?

Geckos have special gripping toe pads, which allow them to walk across ceilings and upside down under branches. DO NOT try this at home!

Mary K Fun Facts

- Chameleons can change colour according to their moods: green - angry, brown - threatened, red - relaxed.

- They really have little power over how they change colour – it's more like the way we blush bright red sometimes.

- If a chameleon is afraid, or a predator is about, it will turn a dark colour to blend into the background.

- Being invisible isn't always useful: if a chameleon is feeling amorous, they turn a bright colour to attract a mate.

Chameleons

Two thirds of all the world's chameleons live in Madagascar. They are a cute, almost comical-looking reptile. BUT THEY ARE NOT AS SLEEPY AS YOU THINK! It takes only .04 of a second for a chameleon to zap an insect for supper.

Now you see it now you don't

A chameleon can stick out its tongue, and roll it back in so quickly, the human eye can't even see it. See the chameleon's tail all curled up? When unravelled their tails are great for balancing high up on the branches of the Malagasy forests.

How long is a chameleon's tongue?
From the tip of its nose to the end of its tail.

A clever little tail

When a lizard is being attacked by a predator, e.g. a big hungry bird, it can lose its tail, confuse the bird and run, run, run. The lizard can later regrow its tail.

Do chameleons have eyes on the back of their heads?

NO, but a chameleon's eyes can move independently of each other. When one eye is looking forward, the other can be checking out what's sneaking up behind!

Lemurs

Lemurs are found in the wild only in
Madagascar. Lemurs are primitive primates
this means they are 'before monkeys',
or prehistoric monkeys.

Why do lemurs only
live in Madagascar?

Lemurs evolved in isolation when Madagascar
broke away from mainland Africa 160 million
years ago. Many of the island's animals evolved
into species seen nowhere else on earth.
Most lemurs are aboreal; they live in trees and
eat flowers, insects, eggs and fruit.

Where do our souls go?

The black and white indri is the largest and one of the most threatened lemur in the world. To see the indri, you must sit very quietly in the forest and wait, wait, wait.

Legend has it that one day a man called Koto and his son went into the forest in search of bananas and honey, but they never returned.

The village people loved Koto so they went to find him and his son. Weeks went by and they searched further and further into the dense rainforest. Eventually up in a tree, they found a lemur they had never seen before – the largest lemur they had ever seen, with a long, loud mournful cry – a cry that travels over 3km (over 1.5m) through the rainforests.

The village people believed that the souls of Koto and his son had been transformed into the indri lemur and vowed never to eat an indri as it could be the soul of their beloved Koto. The long haunted cry of the indri was Koto's lament that he could never return to his village. Hence, the Malagasy name for the indri is, 'babakoto', which means Papa Koto.

Why do ringtailed lemurs sunbath?

Lemurs sit in the sun in a yoga-like position to warm up after the cool Malagasy nights.

Stink fights

Lemurs like nothing better than a good stink fight. The male lemurs wipe their tails with smelly scent from under their arms and stink away rival lemurs. Please do NOT try this at home!

Africa

Kenya

Never travel faster than your angels can fly

If the Masai, one of the African tribes, have to travel long distances, you will see them huddled together in the shade, resting after their journey, waiting for their souls to catch up with them.

Mary K Fun Fact

Cheetah are one of the few members of the cat family to hunt by day. Lions and leopards mostly rest during the day and hunt by night.

Why don't cheetahs wear sunglasses?

Cheetahs have dark line markings under their eyes which absorb the light from the sun so that the cheetah is able to hunt without being blinded by the glare. Sunglasses just aren't practical if y need to run at 100kph (62mph)!

Hippos don't open their huge jaws to laugh; they are showing off their enormous teeth to scare you away!

Where do hippos pooh?

The Masai children say that God created the plant-eating hippopotamus to roam with the elephants, gazelle, giraffe and zebra, but the hippos couldn't bear the scorching sun. They asked God if they could live in the rivers. God said 'no' as the crocodiles would eat them. The hippos replied that they would stay in large groups to be safe. Then God said, 'Look at the size of you! You will eat all the fish in my rivers.'

The hippos promised God that they would live in the rivers by day, but they wouldn't eat any fish. They would come out to eat grass and plants by night.

God wanted to know how He could be sure they were not eating the fish. The hippos came up with a plan: they would always pooh out of the water so that God could check their pooh for fish bones!

This is why hippos live in the water, eat at night and never, never, never pooh in the rivers.

13

Africa
Tanzania

Do crocodiles need toothbrushes?

NO. Crocodiles don't need to brush their teeth because when their teeth fall out they grow another set and their teeth are constantly replaced by lovely large new teeth! But Mary K is no crocodile so she keeps brushing.

Why do crocodiles lie around with their mouths open?

Is this croc waiting around for lunch? NO. Sensitive blood vessels in the crocodile's mouth help keep him cool.

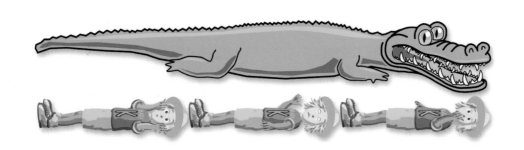

How to survive a crocodile attack

Mary K canoed down the Zambezi, the large river which lies between Zimbabwe and Zambia. Mad Max, Mary K's guide, gave her some advice: 'If you fall into the Zambezi, do not swim to shore as the hippopotamuses will charge and kill you and if you make it to the shore, the wild buffalo will maul you to death, and that's if the crocodiles haven't attacked and eaten you as you swim across the river.'

So Mary K asked what should she do if her canoe capsized?

Mad Max explained: 'Mary K, you must stay with your canoe, because it is the shape of a large crocodile so the hippos and crocodiles won't attack you as they will be afraid of you.'

Mary K still couldn't sleep a wink. In the middle of the night she called to Max who was out keeping watch by the campfire. 'What if there are crocodiles in the Zambezi bigger and longer than my canoe?' Max responded in a sleepy voice. 'Then THOSE crocodiles will kill and eat you. Goodnight!'

Africa

Zimbabwe

Mary K Fun Facts

- After 30 years baobab tree trunks can measure 10m (33ft) in diameter and can store up to 135,900 litres (35,900 gallons) of water.

- The fruit of the baobab is called 'monkey bread' after the monkeys that love to eat it!

Mary K Fun Facts

- One kick from a giraffe's elegant leg could kill you.

- Acacia leaves, the giraffe's favourite food, contain a lot of water so giraffes can go for a long time without drinking.

- When you see a herd of giraffes, usually about 12, they all look in different directions watching out for their predators.

- How long is a giraffe's black tongue? 45cm (18in). You need a very long ladder and to be super quick with your ruler.

- When standing still, the markings of the giraffe make it almost invisible; it looks like a tall brown tree.

The baobab tree can live for 1,000 years.

The upside-down tree

The Masai children told Mary K that God was angry with the baobab tree, because it stored up all the water for itself and wouldn't share. God decided to teach the tree a lesson. He plucked up the huge baobab tree and replanted it upside down. To this day all baobabs look like they are upside down with their roots sticking up towards the sky.

The talking trees

When a giraffe has finished eating at an acacia tree, it doesn't move on to the next tree nearby. Instead it continues eating at trees some distance away. The Ndebele children of Zimbabwe explained that this is because the magic acacia tree lets out a sour juice so that the giraffe no longer finds the leaves so tasty, and then the tree warns all the acacia trees around it that the hungry giraffes are about. And so the giraffe must continue to feed somewhere else.

Note:
Naturalists say the giraffe has 4 stomachs, like a cow, and so needs time between trees to chew the cud. This is why they move so far from tree to tree. Mary K prefers the story of the magic talking trees.

Asia

Asia is the largest continent in the world and is home to almost half of the world's people.

Asian elephant

Elephants are the largest land animals. Their trunks are an extension of their nose and upper lip and are used for smelling, drinking, showering and for greeting other elephants.

Mary K Fun Facts

- The elephant's tusks are actually their massive front teeth.
- The elephant society is matriarchal – mammy is boss.
- Elephants can't jump.

How to survive an elephant charge

1. Stay downwind so they can't smell you.

2. Stand very, very still. Elephants have a 'blind spot' – they might not see you.

3. Run like crazy and take a sharp left at the last minute.

4. Stay at home and hide under your bed!

Bangladesh & Thailand

Bangladesh lies to the east of India. The capital, Dhaka, is one of the most populated cities in the world.

The capital of Thailand is Bangkok. The main religions are Buddhism and Islam.

Bangladesh   Thailand

Far-flung fashion

The main religions in Bangladesh are Islam and Hinduism. Muslims are the followers of Islam. The women wear clothes that cover them from head to toe. In Bangladesh this outfit is called a 'shalwar kamees'; in Afghanistan a similar outfit is called a 'burka'. Hindu women wear a 'bindi', a painted dot, on their foreheads. Once a symbol of marriage and protection, nowadays it is more of a fashion statement.

munu, aged 4

Asia

The Philippines

The Philippines is made up of over 7,000 islands and is separated from the Asian mainland by the South China Sea.

The evil eye

Filipinos greet you by raising and lowering both eyebrows while making eye contact. But staring too hard is thought to be giving one the 'evil eye' and is believed to cause illness.

Smile!

Filipinos smile when they are happy, but they also smile when embarrassed, when criticising, and when they have caused a minor offence!

What are chicken feathers for?

Filipino village houses are made from bamboo and built on stilts to protect them from floods. While visiting one of these houses, Mary K noticed that the family had a collection of chicken feathers stuck into the kitchen ceiling. And what are the feathers for? They are used for cleaning out your ears. DO NOT try this at home!

Cambodia

Cambodia is in Asia, and the capital city is Phnom Penh.

Panha, aged 7

Cambodia

Chicken Village

When Mary K was visiting the remote mountain villages of Cambodia, she came across a place called GUESS WHAT? CHICKEN VILLAGE! Right in the centre of the village stands a 50m (164ft) concrete chicken. The women believe that if they pray to this holy chicken they'll be 'blessed' with a man.

Angkor Wat

Angkor was once the largest city in the world and the capital of Cambodia. Angkor Wat is a vast stone temple city built by the Khmers nearly 900 years ago. The majestic temples honour the Hindu and the Buddhist gods. This fascinating ruined city with its monkey sculptures, hidden turrets and mythology is known as the 'eighth wonder of the world'.

What does 'wat' mean?

'Wat' means 'temple'.

Asia

India

India

With 1 BILLION people, India is one of the most populated places in the world. India's capital is Delhi.

Holy cow

Delhi is a vast, chaotic city with intense air pollution, lively markets, rickety rickshaws and holy cows with good-luck rumps that have right-of-way on the road.

Poacher turns gamekeeper

An Irishman, Jim Corbett, is a hero in Northern India as set up their first national park. Originally he came to these forests at the foot of the Himalayas to kill man-eating tigers. The locals were cutting down the forests farmland, firewood and building, and therefore they wer destroying the tiger's habitat and turning the tigers int maneaters. Jim Corbett was so successful at stamping the tigers that the Indian tiger came close to extinction but then he had a change of heart and put all his knowledge into Save the Indian Tiger. Today the tiger is protected species and can only be killed in self defence.

Holy monkeys

In India the relationship with people, wildlife and the natural world is interwoven with God. The waters, forests and the animals must be respected and protected. Hindus consider all monkeys to be holy; their favourite monkey is the Hanuman langur, which is called after the monkey god, Hanuman, and is a symbol of devotion. The langur monkey is free to live in the Hindu temples and is welcome in the villages and towns.

Corbett National Park

In a country where there is very little space for so many people, it is a tribute to the people that they are prepared to sacrifice land for a national park. The Corbett National Park is home to jackals, Asian elephants, wild boar, chital (or axis deer), pythons, vipers, cobra, langur monkeys and gharial.

What's a gharial?

It's a rare, fish-eating, long-nosed crocodile.

Mary K Fun Fact

In India a flip flop is tied to the back of the rickshaws. WHY? Indians believe that the right side is good so they eat and shake hands with their right hand; they use their left hand to take off their shoes. When their shoes are old and dirty, they tie the left shoe to the back of their rickshaw to keep away evil spirits.

South America

Chile

Unlike the herds of migrating mammals on the plains of Africa, South America has hundreds of species of smaller or more exotic creatures like insects, birds, the red-faced monkey, the dart-poison frog and the giant Galapagos tortoise. Hidden far in the rainforests are creatures yet to be discovered.

Chile

Chile is the longest, thinnest country in the world. The Pacific Ocean lies to the west; Argentina and the Andes, the world's longest mountain range, lie to the east.

Deserting the desert

Mary K put on her woolly pink hat and got on her horse, Jodie, and headed off into the Atacama Desert to see the fantastic and haunting Valley de la Luna and the beautiful Chilean flamingos. The Valley de la Luna (Moon Valley) is so dry and salty that nothing, not even insects, live here. It really is a deserted desert!

When Mary K had photographed the pink flamingos, Jodie suddenly became anxious and jumpy and decided to take off and gallop all the way home. There was no stopping him! SO WHAT WAS UP WITH JODIE? The gauchos told Mary K that there was a storm warning and Jodie, with his highly developed intelligence and instincts, had been desperate to return to the safety of his stable.

Incas

The Incas are the Native Americans who lived in Chile before the Spanish conquerors arrived in the 1530s.

How to survive on a runaway horse

If your horse is a runaway, hold on tightly, as the horse will eventually slow down and stop. Jumping from the back of a speeding horse could cause serious injury. Try and sit back in your saddle as leaning forward encourages your horse to go faster. A horse bolts when it is anxious or afraid so never kick, hit, or scream at a runaway as this will scare the animal even more. Talk gently to your horse and this will help calm him. Once he slows down, dismount immediately in case he bolts again!

South America

Atacama Desert

The Atacama Desert

The driest place in the world is the Atacama Desert of northern Chile. Temperatures can soar by day and plunge by night. Only a few plant and animal species such as flamingos can survive these conditions.

Mary K Fun Facts

- A group of flamingos is called a colony.
- Flamingos make their nests from mud, which helps keep their eggs cool.
- The flamingo's bent beak is perfect for sifting small animals and plants from the shallow water and soggy soil.
- Each flamingo has over 25,000 beautiful pink feathers.

Why do flamingos stand on one leg?

Are they just showing off?
NO. They are resting and conserving heat, keeping one long, bare leg warm at a time.

Venezuela

Caracas is the capital of Venezuela and the Orinoco, the large Venezuelan river, is famed for its white-water rafting.

Venezuela

How to survive a river current

Mary K was very scared when she fell into the Orinoco River and was trapped under her boat, but she remembered what her dad told her when she was learning to swim in Inchydoney. Try to stay calm, float, get your bearings, then use your strength to swim diagonally out of the current, going with the flow not against it. Once out from under the boat, Mary K stayed with the boat for floatation until help came.

N.B: Always wear your life jacket when in a boat.

Galapagos Islands

The Galapagos Islands

The uninhabited Galapagos Islands lie on the equator off the coast of South America and are home to the smallest, rarest penguins in the world, the beautiful blue-footed booby and the prehistoric giant Galapagos tortoise. The islands are named after their unique giant inhabitants. 'Galapago' means 'saddle' in Spanish so the islands are named after the saddle-backed giant Galapagos tortoise.

Blue-footed booby

The blue-footed booby is a famous Galapago seabird, which looks like somebody picked it up and dipped its feet in a bucket of 'powder blue' paint.

re the blue-footed boobies
blue with the cold'?

O. The blue-footed booby has cousins out at sea called the
-footed booby. The colour of their feet is determined by
at they eat. The blue-footed booby eats the fish and
ellfish close to shore and the red-footed booby eats the fish
y out at sea. It's like the pink flamingos. Their diet of
imp gives them their fantastic pink colour.

Mary K Fun Facts

- The blue-footed booby does not build nests; it lays its eggs in a slight hollow in the beaches.

- They have no predators and therefore their eggs do not need a lot of protection.

- The Spaniards called these seabirds 'Bobo', which means clown, after their bizarre courting ritual: they waddle from side to side on their bright blue feet, bend their heads back and point their beaks in the air. Then they do a funky bow and spread their wings out in a strutting routine. The male booby whistles and the female honks.

Frigatebirds

The frigatebirds are an unusual and very distinctive bird. What other bird do you know spends up to 20 minutes blowing up a bright red, football-sized pouch under its beak in order to attract a female.

The pirates of the Galapagos?

Frigatebirds are known as the pirates of the Galapagos. These large black seabirds have the largest wingspan for their size in the world. Their wingspan is so large that they need a little downhill runway to gather the momentum to take flight.

Once in the air the frigatebird acts like a pirate, harrassing smaller birds for their catch of fish. A frigatebird cannot dive for its own fish as its small preening glands are not able to secrete enough oils to make its feathers waterproof and its long wings would not be able to get enough downstroke to take off again from the water.

Mary K Not-so-fun Facts

- Tortoises can live for weeks without water. Over the last two centuries sailors caught these giant creatures and stacked them up in heaps on their ships while they sailed for months out at sea. As the sailors became hungry, they killed the tortoises one by one.

- Today only about 15,000 giant Galapagos tortoises remain, but they are now protected.

Giant Galapagos Tortoise

Tortoises are reptiles; they have changed little since prehistoric times. Its soft vulnerable body is protected by its hard shell.

Mary K Fun Facts

- The giant Galapagos tortoises are the largest tortoises in the world; they can be over 2m (almost 5ft) long.

- They can live for over 150 years.

Mary K Yucky Fact

- The frigatebird often robs the fish of the blue-footed booby. But if the frigatebird is too late for supper, because the blue-footed booby has already eaten his fish, the frigatebird will force the booby to puke the fish back up so he can eat it himself!

Who was Charles Darwin?

Charles Darwin was a scientist who travelled to the Galapagos Islands in 1831. He developed a 'theory of evolution', which explains that the strongest survive.

The marine iguana

The marine iguana is known as the dragon of the Galapagos. It is black with spines on its back and occasionally it puffs clouds of salt out of its nose. According to the seasons and mating times, they can change colour from black to red to blue.

Marine iguanas are the only sea-going lizards to be found in the world. When the islands ran short of food for the iguanas, they had no choice but to turn to the oceans for food. They eat seaweed and have evolved to swim to depths of 12m (almost 40ft) and can actually stay under water for up to an hour.

Mary K Final Fun Facts

- Take only photos; leave only footprints.
- Write a diary of your journeys so that you'll never forget your adventures.

What does evolution mean?

Evolution is to slowly develop and change in order to survive, e.g. if the world, millions and millions and millions of years ago, was flooded Mary K would probably have webbed feet and webbed fingers in order to swim faster.

INDEX

Page numbers in **bold** show where to find pictures.